Awful
LOVELY

DIRTY SWEET POETRY

Awful LOVELY

DIRTY SWEET POETRY

TIFFANY SIMONE

STEWART PRESS PUBLISHING
300 SOUTH MEDIA GROUP
♦♦♦
NEW YORK

You are the story I will always love telling,
but he is my love story come true.

I have a lot of work to do today; I need to slaughter memory, turn my living soul to stone, teach myself to live again.

— Anna Akhmatova

Somehow, you've won.
     You've managed to love me and ruin me all at once.
My mind runs towards you,
     while my sanity circles back, seeking safety.
I want to erase everything and do it all over again.
     That's how good you hurt.

— down the rabbit hole I go

This is an ache,
      an open wound,
         the *worst* case scenario…
      like walking naked into a crowded room.
Lost senses, losing your way, ten consecutive rainy days.
  This is everything you already know, but pray isn't true.
       This is lovers confessing
             they will never EVER be with you.

It's an almost guaranteed matter of addiction.
These words should most certainly stay in our mouths.
Within this silence, there is a *distinct* passion,
        an all too honest level of attraction.
But, you know I can no longer say
      those sorts of **forbidden things** out loud.

— *scandalous*

There's a damp napkin under your vodka and lime,
      a dripping sweaty glass just as empty as mine...
and you can't look away from my eyes.
You'll be gone tonight
    leaving unanswered questions behind,
      and I'll regret thinking
        every little thing was a sign.

Everything is different,
    but I promise *nothing has changed.*
I simply cannot get away from your name.

— *still*

You are an overwhelming sense of desire;
       something perhaps not quite human.
There's a fullness beneath my rib cage.
      I think you are growing within my bones.

Love is a safe word,
      a soft place,
          a rose,
            a scent,
              a breath.
Love is your weak spot,
      your gentle heart,
          with tears and fears
          and sad songs.
Love is everything until it's nothing
      and forgetting is terribly long.

— *the strength in being weak*

ﾟ.✧ ❀ ✧.ﾟ

I'll probably crash trying to get these words out.
You're the pause in the middle of my day.
Not every day, but too many,
enough to make me crazy.
I feel your want like it's something tangible.
You're on the top shelf of my inner pedestal,
and I can't seem to bring you down.
Maybe I like you there.
Maybe you're the reason I've come this far.
Maybe you're the reason I can't seem to go any further. .

— *confessions of a prisoner*

ﾟ+ ✧ ❀ ✧ +ﾟ

You take over and I don't even have time
    to hold my love in,
the way I've taught myself to,
to make my mind blank,
      body calm, flat and numb,
the way I know I need to,
to win…
    or to save myself from losing.

Invite me in.
Show me all the places you've been neglected.
Let's slowly address this recurring sadness.
I think our months might be full of answers tonight.

When these waves come,
     I wonder which part of me will come crashing next.
I hate how sometimes I can put you to rest,
      while others you swim dangerously close,
      a shark in my head.
 I need you dead.

Vividly I remember the kissing...
how I wanted to dive right down your lovely slender throat.
I was a hungry little thing— *a savage in a sundress.*
My mouth was on a mission to deliver you my soul.
I would've slipped under your skin
      if it meant I could take away all that pain.
We were on a quest to see who could love harder.
    You tasted like passion, and I needed to be fed.
I was the hunter,
        the wolf
          and the naïve girl in red.

— girls can be wolves too

Don't find me.
My mind always recklessly decides
             to come to you *first*.
I guess a part of me will always like
 r u n n i n g
 a bit more than
        coming home.

The parking lot. Seeing each other again after all those years. Of course I went.

We were scared of ourselves and each other. I knew your words would still remain liquid smooth.

Though, you were embarrassed and it was cute. But you told me that my eyes were medicinal, that when you looked at me you'd felt genuinely accepted.

Yes, I remember.

I torture and comfort myself with the same memory. The part where I sat in your lap. My moves were bold, but I'd shyly looked away. You'd gently touched my cheek, pulling my face back to yours.

"What?" I asked.

"I need your eyes."

Your low voice had released butterflies into my stomach.

I witnessed you drinking in my adoration. I was more than willing to pour it all over you. You wanted to put me in your pocket.

Keep me close.

Then why do you always leave?

I gave your heart peace. Our love was so comfortable because we found a mutual dark. Bodies lit up, hands, mouths, souls...sparks.

That's just the way it was with us.

Every time.

The parking lot. Of course I'll go.

But I've kept the wounds.

My heart's a stubborn creature,
     with this incessant beating...
wanting everything,
       feeling all of it.
I'm fascinated by the way you want to
       delicately hold,
         yet simultaneously **take a bite out of me.**

Break that kindness all over me.
Pour more passion like rain.
  I begged for this thunder.
And I loved when the lightning came.

To me, **he was the epitome of passion.**
In gaining him,
      I lost myself.
The descent was a blur of colors..
      a dead bouquet of flowers—
        and we were thrown.

Far from each other.
Close to perfection.
Him and I.
Our stories are magnificent.
In my imagination
  we never got out of bed.

Meet me in the field we always talked about.
      I'll wear a long ivory dress
          and "accidentally" forget my panties.
You can whisper words of forever.
      I'll breathlessly call out your name,
       enjoying our little game
          of believing all of the little things we say.

I have these moments,
 these days,
        this odd sickness…
where everything seems too beautiful,
                too sad,
                    just too EVERYTHING.

— *I think I'd rather not be so close to my own heart*

════════ ༶ꙮ୧ᦔ °·✧ ❀ ✧·° ᦔ୧ꙮ༶ ════════

I've been wishing so hard for you to love me,
the way I love you...
but wishes are for fountains and stars,
and I'm just a girl with a big stupid heart.

═══════ ᧬᧬᧬ °.✧ ✿ ✧.° ᧬᧬᧬ ═══════

What you felt like was **sunshine**
         and the memories still flood.
    Like light,
    like the brilliance of your smile with that first look.
There was a time when I understood,
     good things should feel good.
 Happiness is a pocketful of your compliments
        and I wanted to give you all of my thank you's.
My stomach still does flip flops, eyes searching,
               I mean…each passing car *could be.*
 Which one did we make out in on that first night,
   or the last day or the one secret meeting in the parking lot
when you told me baby blue nail polish would always remind you of
my sandaled feet in your lap.
 Remember twinkle lights wrapped around my bed posts…
    because I wanted to fall asleep *to you, with you, on you.*
Instead I live picking out memories like candy and I savor them *until*
I'm sated.
    Worn out. **I've spent too much time in the sun.**

You are my weakness,
  my trigger,
    the safe place *inside my head.*
You are my heartbeat,
  my fountain wish,
    the other side of my empty bed.
With the lights off,
  and a bit of whiskey,
I let myself pretend it's you.
   Arching my back,
     giving into it,
     knowing you have the same dreams too.

I hate your smile...the way it sticks in my brain.
You're like an awkward silence on top of itchy winter skin.
Fill me up and smooth this out,
     because my body hates remembering,
         and I despise pretending.
   I'll admit,
you've always been at the heart of every goddamn thing.

My smile ate your pain— fully (still)…
      in my mind *your mouth runs wild.*
   We are the wounded,
      wondering, *longing* for whispers of forgiveness.
My eyes were too wide and inviting.
   I almost died.
      I hope you get this.

All that I am
 has *everything*
and *nothing* to do with you.

— *in case you were wondering*

I need to put you to bed, and not in the way you may think.
You're keeping me up, restless with memories.
Please go lay in the quieter part of my soul.
Set yourself up in the less used section of my heart.
I'll check on you,
 pinky promise, cross my heart.
I know you know,
>   that that was then,
>   and this is now,
>   and I need a fresh start.
I need some peace.
Release me from the waiting.
Feel comfort in a love that's constant as you drift off.
Imagine my hair draped over you,
>   in a forehead goodnight kiss.
These memories have been precious teachers.
Trust me, you will always be missed.

— *now I lay you down to sleep*

She's more kindness, than fight.
Beauty in such a delicate spirit
making men hunger to be heroes...
    when all along she's been doing the saving.

— *superhero in disguise*

═══════════ ૐ ♪℮ᘰ °·✧ ✿ ✧·° ᘰ℮♪ ═══════════

I may never get used to a kindness like that.
It will always throw me off a bit.
But I think my gratitude shocks him too,
and *I love all the smiling I make his mouth do.*

She was a girl held together by
irrational hope and cheap glue.
She was prone to flights of fancy,
and more than her fair share
 of tears.

══════════ ꙮꙅꙶꙢ °⋅✧ ❀ ✧⋅° Ꙣꙶꙅꙮ ══════════

Perhaps I'm the kind that loves badly.
  With toxicity that shouldn't be passed along.
There are too many demons wrapped around me.
Anything and everything will always be wrong.
Hands devouring skin,
contradicting the way my eyes drag you right in
Strangled and tangled
haunted with doubt

Romantic or not, the writer in me turns wicked on paper.
I'll wear baby pink when I hurt you.

You did bad things,
and now the good life will be nothing but a dream.
You're the nightmare
that made a mean girl live in me.

— *bitter*

She's the kind of girl you don't let go of.
She's a firecracker that one,
a combination of hell yes and fuck no.
Hang on, because whatever it is,
you want it.
She's desire...
all love,
passion and fire.

— *the total package*

She's a vice,
    an addiction,
       a blessing mixed with tragedy.
Women that taste of sincerity and sin are like that...
    Suddenly you're smiling,
       but you're crazy.

He was like hunger at night,
      all passionately right,
    with love notes whispered or screamed,
          depending on us,
             and well...*everything.*
I wanted him in a way that was so much bigger than desire.
 So, I nicknamed him Fire,
         and we burned.

— *hot*

He only came to me when he was hungry
for love confessions.
But, for him
      I had nothing more to give.
Unfortunately, this time
he was going to have to *starve.*

Everything about you had been so smooth.
 Your mouth, a bit too welcoming,
with words that had the power to soothe...
And when you kissed me, *you'd growled.*
 It was like something wild inside desperately needed out.
Your desire was so furious,
and I ached for that ravenous sound.

There's a screaming silence in feelings this naked.
I'm spelling out R E A D Y
  with nervous fingertips
 into your skin.
  (*as my heart skips*)
To be honest, *I don't know what's happening.*
Love's present, yet I'm begging to hide in it.

— *apologizing with my body*

Closing my eyes...
I'm not sure if you're a memory,
 a burden or a lullaby.

She remembers your smile.
She remembers your face.
She remembers
  how the lines of your body felt like moments;
  moments she'd *needed*.
And everything missing became all that there was,
and everything empty exploded into love.

It all washes over me in the shower.
 I attempt a reprieve, *an escape from my brain.*
Craving that one second of relief until I'm drowning again.
There's one clear moment— then *I can't breathe.*
Words repeat patterns in the form of pounding headaches.
Little girl, little girl. I'm breaking in.
 I'm breaking in.

I hope you see this vulnerability for what it is.
Brave.
True.
Sexy, raw and revealing.
> *Hear me getting naked for you.*

— *stripped*

I worried that I would taste like despair if you kissed me for too long.
I wondered if this was simply something bittersweet.
But you continue to look at me as if I'm a place of worship,
    your eyes all desperate and full of greed.

— and he whispers, "Down on your knees."

I'm too tired for this ache to exist anymore.
The memory of you is like a slow death.
I still remember how your eyes almost killed me before.

— *murderer*

Her eyes were fucked up shades of green...
kryptonite and jealousy.
Buckle up Baby.
This is the end of your sanity.

Here's the plan.
We'll have passion wrapped in bed sheets.
Completely sick with fevers, from love and other wild things.
Sex like erotic poetry.
Loyalty in our stomachs,
      like a string that connects us.
Perfectly.
 You and me.

— good ideas

═══════════ ꙮ ༄ °᠂ ✧ ✿ ✧ ᠂° ༄ ꙮ ═══════════

I'm the girl spilling my guts out.
Living life, but feeling like my skin's off.
I'd like to remain calm and slip into something sexy,
but I wear these emotions so fucking messy.

— ugly honest

She wears her vulnerability like lingerie...
all beautiful and exposed.
The problem is,
she really wants to take it off.

I will only love you from far away,
 with no sound, and no touch.
We are ink to paper.
 It's so much safer.
Mind steady and heart focused.
In my imagination is the healthiest way.

It's how I'll carry my old stories of you.

───────── ᗢᗢᒪᆷ °. ✧ ❀ ✧ .° ᆷᗢᒪᖴ ─────────

I don't want to be in confusion with you.
I think we need to make a plan…
more randomly making out,
less incessantly picking at nothing.
Just solid, unbreakable love
    where forever doesn't seem long enough.

On my best days
 I let you hold me.
I go to kiss you
 because my stomach tells me to.
My brain turns off
and I'm just the girl in the striped dress again.
I choose us
 and I'm desperately in love with your hands.

Because I was a giver…
  and I said sweet things
  and I was willing
  and I heard you…
Yet, you only reached for me *when I left.*

Let the shadows come **because I am no longer afraid.**
I don't feel the pull of the waves quite as much
with your heart holding onto me like that.

— *lifesaver*

I don't meet halfway, *I demand.*
It's colder here but you still come to bed.
Before we get lost in the land of too— far— gone,
you should know…
you were exactly what I was asking for.
I guess pain can come in the form of little blonde girls.

We lived caught up in the moment
Calling chaos *beautiful*
Pushing down the obvious truth…
You only think I'm pretty because
this love is torturing you.

Maybe you still live in that moment too...
remembering how my eyes set you free
      and held you all at once.
I called your smile a love song, impossible to forget.
We are a melody stuck on repeat in my heart.
He craves me so intensely.
Even when I'm alone
     I feel like I'm surrounded by his want.

I'll be forever walking with these knives in my back,
      hunched over from the pain of your non— love.
My heart weighs more than my body
      and I'm completely aware that when I ache,
           you feel nothing at all.

Bleeding through these lines,
     with scars coming apart at the seams...
It's like my healing hasn't amounted to anything.
     I'm only half awake, but fully aware.
I'm an agitated clock ticking backwards.
Itchy with feelings falling out,
I've come undone.
My skin's stopped doing its job of protecting me,
   just like
  your love has stopped doing its job of never leaving.

— *you're fired*

I was starvation,
and you hated to eat.
I became the prayer that had you down on your knees.
A soft place when you'd refused sleep.
I can dance fondly with these toxic memories,
but quitting you is the poetry in me.

— retired

Creeping in like the low rumble of a thunderstorm.
The air's heavy with hints,
                    telltale signs.
This is something bigger than us.
        And suddenly we're drenched.
You admitted you were anger
I told you I was rain…
but in the end
we both still stayed.

There will be this.
  Here.
There will be my running and your reaching.
It'll be soft and quiet,
 and then a sudden, overwhelming
                  all at once.
Know this.
  Here.
          Baby, either way...*it is us.*

— *true story*

Undress me.
Undress you.
Look fear in the eyes and kiss me too.
This will be like nothing before.
This will be like nothing else *ever again*.

There was something about his voice
 that made me smile **crazy...**
a girl all heart eyes and hungry hands.
I want to be her again.
Sanity is overrated.

You look like a dreamer,
but I'm a stealer of peace.
I devour your smiles like they're nothing to me.
 I'm a maker of nightmares, not as good as I look.
Bad equals bad here,
I'm the mistake you mistook.
My lying eyes are a little too wide.
"Believe me I'm innocent," the guilty girl said.
It's really only a matter a time,
they only say yes.

When we slip away from it all,
        I remember myself underneath.
I am less windy.
My mind's at rest.
That's where I wish to live
   and where my love thrives
     at its best.

Your love is so powerful—
it kills the part of me
that hates the feel of good.

━━━━━━━ ༄ ♆ °. ✧ ✿ ✧ .° ♆ ༄ ━━━━━━

You only love me when I cooperate,
       when I say "YES",
when I pretend that the big things mean nothing to me.
       But I loved you on all the days.

So, now I'm this feisty girl saying "NO",
       And "fuck that."
EVERYTHING means *everything* to me.

— *feisty*

I shouldn't have wandered so close to the edge of unreasonable.
Perhaps I'm being somewhat of an unlovable Love.
You used to hold on with an unwavering certainty
Now I'm certainly slipping away.
I thought you'd understand...
I'm unfamiliar with sweet things.
Damnit, these cravings hurt.

— *love sick*

I probably shouldn't like this pain,
  but I'm a *sick little monster,* so, I do.
A clever pretender,
   you know I'll surrender.
Take care of me,
   make it better.
 I'm the beauty, you're the beast.
Ridiculously hungry, I'll be your feast.
Darling, this part of my heart may be a bit darker
   than you're used to.

After the desert I found you.
Dehydration had driven me mad.
You were a man on a mission, *a beautiful opportunity*,
with desire dripping from the palms of your hands.
I was eager and you went down smoothly, like water. Without
questioning I drank cup after goddamn cup of all that you offered.
We justified our weaknesses and rationalized our games. I wanted to
believe in fate and fairy tales because of the undeniable way I had fit
against your body.
The second we'd connected it was like the world opened up. Your
voice grew daisies in my stomach. *You were my butterflies.*
You ate my skin.
I was exactly what you needed, and temptation did us in.
True love is patient, but we'd clearly lost our minds.
Reality came as a shock, like wildfire.
Discovering we couldn't be anything, turned everything into nothing
and nothing was ever bright again.

— I was dying of thirst and you were the only thing I wanted in my
mouth

All of the bursts of light tonight will be you.
Wish after wish after wish…
Memories,
    laughter,
       and the feel
          of your fingertips—
            against my wrists.
And my appreciation will sound like thunder.

— fireworks

Maybe we can become one of those love stories
        that people dream of...
the kind you're almost positive doesn't exist.
Let's become something so precious
        that we're continuously falling.
I'll stay beside you with green eyes inviting,
        and hands promising *I'm your girl.*
Baby, let's surprise ourselves,
        and then, **we'll shock the world.**

— *couple goals*

All the life you've lived is your truth—
and every day you get to decide...
has the past given you wings
                              or poisoned you.

— *breaking cycles*

I wasn't even there in real life,
 I was there in my mind.
And still, to this day,
that's enough to make me smile.
The wrong direction,
is the road I like to drive from time to time.

— *wanderlust*

Let me hear your nighttime desires
     revealed in broad daylight.
Don't deny me the beauty of such feral liberations.

— *nocturnal animals*

To look at you equals breathlessness,
a desperation.
I just want to tell you one more time.

— *moments of weakness*

I suppose there's that matter of forever,
  but you feel like ever and ever...
a blood spill,
an infection,
 something fucking relentless.
 Haunting me seems to be what you do for a living,
I'm aware you'll never NOT be a part of my history,
But the past doesn't need resurrecting,
and I won't go to sleep with ghosts anymore.

— *recovery*

I've got a bad habit of putting you on
 when I shouldn't be anywhere close to your memory.
Cuddling up with your voice in my mind,
     my clouded head hits the pillow,
          I'm completely broken,
     collapsing in total exhaustion.
These bones are rubbed raw
     from a love that clashes with hate.
I hope you feel awful.
      Just kidding,
          I fucking hope you feel great.

It didn't get easier,
    it got different.
Walking…
     a little bit lost,
and stumbling all too often,
    I discovered all the ways a heart can ache.
But I figured out a way to build my life around the pain.

I went to bed wishing for you *bad*.
With an ache so great it ruined all hope for peace.
You're a need that makes life seem impossible to lead.
I picture you.
Stitching together every thought, piece by piece.
Whispering to the dark, ``**It feels the same for me**.''
And you wonder why.
And you wish you'd tried.

He lays there, faking sleep.
Sometimes the pain is so bad it feels like an aching sickness.
Perhaps a fever.
He thinks he's got a fever.
After all, he isn't the kind to let his emotions get the best of him.
But there are the cravings, and the nightmares.
He's learned to hate the dark; *to hate his heart.*
Whispering, "I don't know what to do with this."
There's a regret that rages deep.
Inside he weeps.

Maybe it's not the good I fear,
 perhaps it's the explosion the two of us *could be.*
All I've ever known is chaos and wildfire,
then falling,
    and failing.
Happiness goes too fast.
It's terrifying how your smile,
              plus, my smile
                   might equal a crash.

— *trauma response*

On certain days she's like the sun.
If you get too close,
especially with a love like that...
you'll burn.

— *protect yourself*

I see the real you,
 and it makes me want to peel myself open and *let you tear me apart.*

I'm your story,
     your wonder,
          your forever and again.
In all your quiet moments,
       I'm loud,
          and dressed in red.
Perhaps, I'm just that little *something*
     keeping love safe
          inside your head.

Let's let it slip away, pleasantly...
like silk falling off,
    like waves receding,
      a war ending,
          the battle retreating.
 You're an internal struggle my mind keeps repeating.
 Reaching out sometimes— stupidly hopeful.
It's messed up.
 My days seem distorted.
I'm being inappropriate.
You should've loved me.
    But maybe *you're* not wrong.
I fear I may have been unworthy all along.

- I'll continue searching for you in everything.

I am not a question of take it or leave it.
I'm a definite YES,
a solid,
clear as day,
 fucking THANK YOU.

— *you're welcome*

October brings leaves in every mood.
A season BOLD in its temperament.
Fierce, yet delicate,
with a glowing light covering an ugly truth.
I suppose you could call me an October too.

— *scorpio season*

You walk around with your stories
that unfold gently from your mouth.
But I am an
E A R T H Q U A K E.
Passion needing out.

...and sometimes everyone's collective energy will sit right on top of
your shoulders.
You'll try to turn your gaze to safe places
    and repeat words of peace,
        but the weight will remain *so damn heavy.*
Exhaustion devours empathetic souls.
You must learn to rest,
        to save the whole.

— learning to save yourself

꧁ ｡ ⋆ ✧ ❀ ✧ ⋆ ｡ ꧂

You're talking to my thighs,
     whispers nipping at my waist.
My skin is now covered in your confessions.
Devotion's kissed fiercely all over my face,
     while I moan eagerly into your mouth.
 I hear your heartbeat,
      as I wait for love's salvation to drip into my veins.

— *making love*

I fell for all the wrong ways,
        everyone destined to leave.
We repeat what we know.
We search and we can't believe.
I may forever falter, but I know **I deserve my day.**

— self awareness

He takes ownership for things that aren't his to hold onto.
You don't need this.
(I want it.)
Words gone round and round.
Passion dripping from tired lashes.
His patience is remarkable.
I promise, nothing goes unnoticed.
And I say thank you *in all the ways*.
With my tears.
With my eyes.
With my body.
And my goodnights.
With every precious sigh.
In time I'm drunk on consistency,
and my reluctance gives way to a confident smile.

You were so scared to sit close to me..
like you didn't trust your heart,
  or your hands.
Unzip your skin and let me in.
That's how close I want to be.

The teeth in my brain are like a creature too afraid
     to take even the smallest of steps.
Secretly I wept.
 Though I am tempted to crawl
     because of this gnawing need
     to hang on to the moans you endlessly create.
The soft flesh of my delicate inner thigh cries words
     to your tongue
     inviting biting and breathless sighs.
Arching back,
     hair splayed,
     hands gripping sheets of our body heat,
 take me to the place where I will confidently know things.
There's waves and stars,
     then electricity shocks my heart
        as I yell out in response.
     Some days I swear,
          you must be a magician.

I walked into you *without any hesitation.*
You were warm summer rain,
and I'd been playing like a crazy girl,
running towards tornadoes
and dancing in lightning storms.

— how refreshing

My mouth carries a secret.
Listen close.
I'm telling time by the way my breath slows.
And I know it sounds sad
 but those of us that know, just know.
You must break and spill before your mind can recognize...
there really is so much strength in these bones.

Unpoetic,
   raw and bruised,
      crying ugly honest,
        out of breath
          and curled up into you..
while I'm reaching for
 and fighting against your love
       ALL AT ONCE—
      that's when my heart's telling
      the WHOLE truth.

— *naked*

There are us,
    the ones that can only stand to be partially seen,
 piece by piece.
Wincing,
     gradually forward, then back again,
 a slow dance, an opposite magic trick, *or sleight of hand.*
Human mysteries,
       wonderful catastrophes,
          disasters we endearingly call *Lovely.*

— *silly nicknames*

Apparently, *I will always be two,*
      one restless, one still…
    messy but neat,
       broken while healing,
        a sad girl, *yet sweet.*
I will always be two,
        the sinner, the saint.
A bitch to love,
       and the lover you hate.

Love is different now...
it's a thankful sacred fire,
and for the life of me
 I don't know how to live with such warmth.

— **coming in from the cold**

All of my ends have split;
  my edges dulled to nothing.
  I believe I've come undone.
Please bring your bigger than mine hands,
  and gently hold my face.
Kiss me like you do
  when you *bring me back to safe.*

When I cannot sleep,
  he does this calm voice, tucking hair behind my ear thing.
I am somewhere in— between awake and dreams.
The edges blur,
        my worried mind scatters to pieces
                and everything important sits still for a moment.
Call me back with your wild, generous mouth.
  Only you have the power to whisper my wounds quiet.
        I will welcome the help and *let us be.*

Thank you for not asking,
      for just knowing,
            for caring and for understanding.
Thank you for not even letting me think
             that I'd be walking this road alone.
          Anymore.

I knew exactly what I was saying.
I spoke straight to his eyes.
My body was ahead of my words,
but my mind and my heart were on time.
Dressed in his red t— shirt he laid me down,
not only was there the revelation of love,
but his pleasant surprise,
because I whispered it *first*.

— *"I love you", I really do*

Take me far, far away from here.
Make me stop feeling my heart.
We can float on blessings and stars.
      Pull my hair,
          tie my hands.
I want to give up some control...
          naked, in our own...
        forever better land.

— *solace*

Wake me up knowing
        exactly how I like my coffee,
because darling,
        mornings aren't for talking.
Open windows and the perfect breeze,
        arching into hands full of greed,
I'm pouty,
   whiny,
      happy,
        knowing I'm your favorite *everything*
          any time of day.

— in bed you can call me princess

Some people can do it.
Some can walk amongst the hurtful and not feel the pain.
I, on the other hand,
     when letting old demons tiptoe closer,
have bravery that goes frozen,
     and a heart *that bleeds me dead.*

My body likes talking to yours,
  with this move and with that,
    with a kiss *here,*
    and a kiss *there,*
      with green eyes carefully dedicating
        through love languages unheard of.
          In my naughty mind I'm licking you everywhere.

The thing is, we often talked about *one day*. Our conversations used to circle back to *fate* and *someday* and *what if* and *possibly*. Round and round like a carousel…we made ourselves sick with the sadness of it all. Like a game, I felt set up. You never showed. *It still feels cold.* I don't want to remember the song of you. You are the lyrics, title long forgotten but words automatic.

And he knows. You must wonder about him and us and the life that we lead. How our days fit together.

How he knows me.

But, the things is, I used to tell you everything. You only fed me bites. I spoiled you. I was the cake.

The whole damn delicious decadent cake.

I gave you every damn piece.

But, he's the cake. He isn't a puzzle. There is no solving anything. It's simple. It's easy.

I'm not scared for my heart. I'm not shaking. And maybe he's not a song, but he's a blanket. And I'm tired of feeling sick and lost…and alone. It's comforting.

He's not you.

 But he's love.

The thing is, I do think some poetry has left me.

But…

the thing is, *I think there's some poetry in coming home.*

—————— ࿐ ೕ ৎ ೫ °⋆✧ ❀ ✧⋆° ೫ ࿐ ৎ ೕ ——————

Tell me anything.
Tell me something.
    Give me good thoughts to dream about.
Say I'm more than pretty,
    because that's how you see me;
       maybe it's the way that you know my mouth.
Just give me words,
    to keep like diamonds,
      for when the silence is too much.
So, tell me anything,
    just tell me something...
      true words I'll believe
        without a doubt.

If first love had a color,
>
> it would be twinkle lights *(just like that night).*

If mistakes had a face,
>
> I'd have a hard time deciphering all the eyes.

If passion was fire,
>
> there'd be scars all over my heart.

But all my thank you's are secretly yours.

Fate tastes like peach sangria,
>
> and FINALLY feels like toes in the sand
>
> > *(where I'm holding your hand).*

If forever love has a color,
>
> I'd call it 'sunrise'.

If there's anything I can give you,
>
> **I'd like to give you KIND.**

He loved me hard and fast,
     with everything, and without pause.
But I fell differently...
     inch by inch,
      needing more,
       my heart beating—
       Because
        Because
        Because.

I had a dream you had surprised me.
You became someone that had wanted me.
Not only were your hands greedy
but your heart was *fucking starving for my love.*

 Bless you for loving me hard enough
to let me sit,
    to let me heal,
       to let me come back together.
The most beautiful thing you can do for another human being is to
not only treasure their heart
      but *to care for their mind.*

There'll remain an everlasting ache
 in the place where you should have spent more time.
But memories can't feed me for the rest of my life…
and the future is abundant
with feelings I've never tried.

All it took was one person saying she was gorgeous.
She could hear how easily it slipped from his tongue,
            and she knew *that's what she wanted...*
WORDS she didn't have to ask for,
 ATTENTION she didn't need to demand,
            and somebody that SAW HER
                    as worth the wait.

— *love languages*

I will hold your heart in such a way
that you will never question
the power of this devotion.

It's not just that I love you...
it's that when I'm scared,
I WANT YOU.
When I'm sad,
I WANT YOU.
And when I'm happy,
I WANT YOU TOO.
Maybe we could hold hands throughout the best
and worst of it.
I know we could live without each other,
but maybe we shouldn't.

— *plans*

I think you'd be surprised at the quiet
when my walls come down
and I allow it...
The release.
The sigh.
The complete letting go
and my giving in.

— *subtle*

She was like a fireworks show
   with all those beautiful colors.
     To know her, was to love her even
            when the sky went black...
      and honestly,
        she could make the dark look damn sexy.

I've taken the road less traveled...
driven off the beaten path,
swerved in and out of traffic
and rediscovered my laugh.
Break rules with me.
Let's change lives and believe.
Just because I've lived with destruction doesn't mean
I don't know
happiness IS the ultimate plan.

I'm in between the believing,
the trusting,
and the giving up.
Discovering how love comes in all the colors, *like the sky.*
Without the dark,
we wouldn't know the light.
And the truth is,
we look so much prettier with desire in our eyes.
We weren't made to let sadness lead our way.
I want to live being proud of my heart,
and the way that it behaves.

Someone will see you...
    and out of all the incredible things,
        your big giant heart
        will be what turns them on the most.

I want a life of love notes and dirty jokes.
In the morning,
   tell me I'm fucking beautiful.
Feed me chocolate.
      Kiss me well.
Let our love remain patient,
      honest and *sexy as hell.*

This is something so good for me,
    I almost don't know what to do with myself.
So, I leave my faith in your hands,
    and let my body fall into your mouth.

— *collapse*

This journey has been laid out before us.
I have held hearts and hearts have held me.
Some have felt like waterfalls, or twinkle lights,
    butterflies and giant smiles.
Him or her, to the point of nothing matters anymore,
    except souls.
And I'll write the chapters that keep calling.
Nothing's easy.
The love of youth is sweet.
Forever love is called Devotion.
You are a choice, and here we go.
It's right and we just know.

You picked out my dress.
    It was always something girly.
I tied my hair up
      so that your eyes would go directly to my neck…
     making you crave my skin,
        making it hard for you to focus.
Because seeing that I was your weakness
      was my absolute favorite thing to notice.

I'm learning to make peace
  with this wandering spirit of mine.
     Serenity comes from my grace and acceptance.
  Life is best lived in the not knowing.
And though I'd like to steer my fear away from the edge,
        bravery breaths understanding.
Falling freely is where the love grows.

— *dive*

Sweetness and fire,
        poetry and sin,
you whisper your heart to me and *I'm ready to begin.*
  With this stirring of butterflies,
        and kind light I'm bathing in,
         you're welcome to my soul and all of this skin.

— *a giver by nature*

It was startling...that look of love.
　　Over time I've learned to wear my chaos well,
　　　but love looks so much better on me.

— *brighter*

Reckless and wild…
 We craved each new second.
We drenched ourselves in
            young
                  stupid
                        hope.
      And it was gorgeous.

There's the ebb and flow of us, like the tide
and we're lost.
I hurry as you stop.
I'm running, but you're not.
Our days end in rain pouring down my face.
I crave the flames.
We float in feelings and unfair games.
I miss breathing in the sunshine
and the freedom of our own wild chase.
Lovers at sea, but we don't...

-

— *drowning*

It seems as if life is a series of revolving doors.
Our biggest decision being, who we let stay,
                              and who we let go...
Our minds ponder questions
      while our mouths give over— complicated answers...
 but truthfully, **we already know.**
Love will be a panic attack of the mind,
                        every time,
                              until it's the right time.
            Our souls tell us so.

— *signs*

Perhaps,
    words were only ever supposed to be words.
The beauty of us having nothing to do with art.
Maybe it was all
    just butterflies
        and sunset…
            an illusion.

I *swear* I think (I probably) didn't know…
Perhaps I should've stopped
  as recklessness tipped straight back down my throat.
Such euphoria, thrilling…openly begging for pleasure.
Your arms were like stumbling into some sort of treasure.
And we wasted our *one good shot.*
But I was greedy,
    binging
      and needy.
I swear, I think (I probably) didn't know.

— *accidentally on purpose falling into trouble*

I want to live in your smile
  the one you said you hated
the one I immediately loved.
It was a random Thursday
  a million summertimes ago.
But my breath still catches
  remembering the bashful way you ducked your head
  when you saw my face.
And so I fell right into your lap the minute you asked.
It was our joke but it didn't feel funny
  because feeling bad felt too good.
And I'm sure I talked too fast,
   flirty words stumbling over and back.
Our entire situation was *awful and lovely,* a blatant fact.
Remembering the shape of your heart
        and weight of your arms,
    I realize this is pointless.
Because there's the way that you tilted my chin,
  and then there's the way that you never did it again.

Some days I wish I'd never met you.
Some days I hate that we held eyes and locked hands.
You healed something that was broken,
     right before deciding not to stay.
Some days I'm so thankful I met you.
Some days I walk forward without out trying to run away.

My skin lights up for you.
Skin welcoming
Mouth eager
Back arched
Mind roaming
Love, help me as I come home.

Like a rose covered in thorns,
      she's a darling in her difficulty.
Something *awful lovely.*
Kissing then biting in the very next breath.
Reaching then fighting,
   simultaneously hot, while freezing to death.
You can come closer,
      but she'd prefer to reach for you instead.
Love carefully, love slowly.
 Fragile things need patience with their unfolding.

The ache in the loss,
the pain with the cravings…
We are indescribable.
There are no comparisons.
You look at me and I forget the world.

As long as you try to silence the scream of my memory
there will always be this war within you.
So run far and fast.
　　　Love is madness,
and your body is still craving a chance.

There are wounds here to uncover.
There are things she will never know how to show.
You must learn to be okay with it,
         the joy of figuring it out as you go.
This is the softness and weak.
But this is the reckless and scary.
She'll have you down on your knees.
In love with her dark will be the best and worst part.
Loving a wild thing is about *cradling a heart.*

And sometimes it really shocks you,
the realness of it all…
the fact that you've made it this far,
  surviving on hope and no fucking clue.
I only know where I'm going
  by *running from where I've been.*
   My strengths in making my own home.

You probably wish I was the kind of girl
    that knew how to smile at roses.
But I'm bad at flowers.
I will never be the oh so sweet one.
I dare you to hold onto me
    with both hands knowing you might bleed.

— *bad flower*

There was that time we took it too far.
It wasn't even dark.
We simply couldn't stop ourselves
Everything fell together,
but at the same time fell apart
You said you couldn't take it anymore.
You wanted closer to my heart
You're my hero and the villain, the beginning and the end.
I'd honestly start all over,
just to stop it all again.

AUTHOR'S NOTE

Sharing my words gives a voice to feelings I've previously been afraid of. Expressing myself creatively has greatly increased my confidence while challenging thoughts of self doubt. The journey takes us far from where we began. Writing is what woke me up. Life is evolving, and I've grown. I'm experiencing a happiness that, honestly, terrifies me. But, as the saying goes, everything worth doing is on the other side of fear. It's time for my next chapter. So, after seven years, Dirty Sweet Poetry will now come to a close. I want to thank you so much for all the support and love you've shown throughout this time. It has meant more to me than you could ever imagine. I will continue to be on Instagram, writing with a renewed vulnerability, as myself, Tiffany Simone.

Follow Dirty Sweet Poetry & Tiffany Simone

Facebook.com/dirtysweetpoetry
Instagram.com/dirtysweetpoetry

Other Titles From Tiffany Simone

Butterflies & Skin: Dirty Sweet Poetry

_____

Beauty In The Let Go: Dirty Sweet Poetry

_____

Pretty Savage: Dirty Sweet Poetry

ACKNOWLEDGMENTS

I was hoping for some sort of closure, knowing full well you'd always be at the heart of me.
But, closure only truly comes with the acceptance that there will never really be any.

Awful Lovely gave me an opportunity to realize there's a beauty to releasing the dark truths that haunt you. The process of writing this book brought forth a light. I was flooded with emotion I wasn't prepared for.
Helping me every step of the way was Jay Long of Stewart Press Publishing, 300 South Media Group. Jay, I am so thankful for your endless patience, basically on demand library sessions and especially for seeing me as an artist, as well as an equal. I thoroughly enjoyed working with you.
On a daily basis, there are two women whose strength is unmatched. Stacy and Sam, you both literally make my brain work. Your presence in my life has changed me.
Andrew, in such a short time you've taught me about mindfulness and grace. I feel incredibly blessed to know you.
I'd also like to thank all of my coworkers for listening to me vent. Each of you brings a perspective all your own that I value and respect.
To my children, all four of you amaze me. One day you'll be old enough to read my words and I hope you smile. Everything is for you.
Lastly, Jacob. Thank you for loving me without judgment, without squeezing too tight. Most likely I'll never believe your kind words, but I adore you for letting me write my heart out in all its crazy glory.

www.ingramcontent.com/pod-product-compliance
Lightning Source LLC
Chambersburg PA
CBHW071152120626
46546CB00006B/2224